The Only Gardening I Do Is When I Give Up

poems by

Thomas Fucaloro

Finishing Line Press
Georgetown, Kentucky

The Only Gardening I Do
Is When I Give Up

Copyright © 2022 by Thomas Fucaloro
ISBN 978-1-64662-933-6 First Edition
All rights reserved under International and Pan-American Copyright Conventions. No part of this book may be reproduced in any manner whatsoever without written permission from the publisher, except in the case of brief quotations embodied in critical articles and reviews.

ACKNOWLEDGMENTS

Brooklyn Poets Anthology ~ "100 Dead People Nobody Misses"
Destigmatized: Voices for Change ~ "Rid Yourself of Doubt . . . Or Should You?"
FIVE:2:ONE ~ "How to Do Everything at Once"
Carcinogenic Poetry ~ "Why Hawaii and Norway Are Not Near Each Other," "Cooking for the Paralyzed"
In Between Hangovers ~ "Backpacking for Shut-Ins," "Peace of Mind by Losing Complete Control for 16 Hours a Day"
E·ratio Poetry Journal ~ "A Complete List of Everyone's Personal Effects"
Quail Bell Magazine ~ "64 Good Reasons for Giving Up Hope"
The Rainbow Project ~ "600 Ways to Give People the Shaft"

Publisher: Leah Huete de Maines
Editor: Christen Kincaid
Cover Art: Julie Bensten
Author Photo: Kristopher Johnson
Cover Design: Elizabeth Maines McCleavy

Order online: www.finishinglinepress.com
also available on amazon.com

Author inquiries and mail orders:
Finishing Line Press
PO Box 1626
Georgetown, Kentucky 40324
USA

Table of Contents

How To Give People Your Best Regards 1
Understanding People You Will Never Meet 2
100 Dead People Nobody Misses 3
How to Do Everything at Once 4
How To Wave Goodbye Without Moving Your Arms 5
Reorganizing Your Pockets 6
124 Simple Exercises for The Teeth 7
Fill Your Life with Croutons 8
Backpacking for Shut-Ins 9
6 Ways to Fuck Up Before Breakfast 10
There's Big Money in Staying Put 11
64 Good Reasons for Giving Up Hope 12
Controlling Fear Without Getting Frightened 13
How to Give Yourself A Complete Physical Without Getting
   Undressed 14
Famous People Who Were Wiry 15
Peace of Mind by Losing Complete Control For 16 Hours a Day 16
I Suck-You Suck 17
600 Ways to Give People the Shaft 18
Apartment Hunting for Devil Worshippers 19
How To Fillet A Panda 20
Rid Yourself of Doubt...Or Should You? 21
Cooking for The Paralyzed 23
A Complete List of All the Things That Are Still Pending 25
A Treasury of Poorly Understood Ideas 26
Your Shoes Are Worth Money 27
Things No One Can Help 28
How To Turn Unbearable Pain Into Extra Income 30
A Complete List of Everyone's Personal Effects 31
I Gave Up Hope and Died and It Worked 32
Why Hawaii And Norway Are Not Near Each Other 33

The titles of these poems are from the George Carlin List Poem "Welcome to The Book Club." These poems, however, are not about George Carlin or that poem and are original works by me

How to Give People Your Best Regards

(Before opening)

Let them know you care
about their well-being and
cranberries upon croutons of good
fortune and salad dressing dreams.

Tell them your hopes, include them
because what's hope without sharing
in the bask of someone else's glow
can you hand me your phone, I want
to let someone else know that their
light can be felt by every last single
one of us and we can't help but project
passion in the form of flame.

Tell them to leave the porch light on.
Loud enough so everyone can hear it.

(This)

Understanding People You'll Never Meet

What are typical questions you would ask
when a ghost is speaking through you?

If I fall in the forest, can you feel it in Minnesota?

How much are lightbulbs anyway?

If you are moving at the speed of light
but forget to tie your shoe
can you trip through sound?

Can you show me the forest you want to fall in?

Why can I always feel it in my belly?

Is it Oreos or wine or ghosts?

Why is understanding people you will never meet difficult?

Why is understanding people you will meet difficult too?

100 Dead People Nobody Misses

I stole the rabbit from the hat
long before it was numerically
valued and processed by time.

I never intended for this
but what's intention without the surprise
of preparation you forgot to intend for?

100 dead people and nobody misses
their strung-out bodies strung up
for no other reason but to turn away.

The overdose is clear and clean
like a law and order episode,
the opioid addiction in this country

begins in how we list things
in priority of what makes sense
but still makes us solve for x.

This poem is the 3rd reason
I decided to wake up today.

How to Do Everything at Once

Stand still. Stiller. Move slow
feeding poison to ducks
that belly up, head down
mentality of movement
can shine but never glow.
Did you scream that? I couldn't
hear you over the almost
creeping into my room,
oh, these deadly cull candles
that dim. Hope enters
and pisses in the corner
and punches the person
sitting next to you.

How to Wave Goodbye without Moving Your Arms

It takes wings

and the urge

to say good-

bye. Did I

pull a muscle

or have you been

running through

my mind and giving me

panic attacks all day?

Reorganizing Your Pockets

My day to day I keep waist-side, holstered,
steadied, and full of lint. My pockets are
where I hide my anxiety at work or play
these fingers fumble into fists furious
with time and how marching to the beat
of a different mental health condition
would be easier than pulling out satchels
of hair with these cloth mittens; Levi's
has the market cornered with *Anti-Anxiety-
Mittens*™ and I hope for royalties
but that is another mental health condition
entirely.

124 Simple Exercises for the Teeth

Anxiety being the hardest substance
in the human body essential for chewing
on speech made from calcium phosphate
rock hard pulp'd chew nerves, layers
of connective tissue that bind roots firmly
to the gums, tissue that helps hold
the teeth, mountain, tightly, against
the jaw.

Fill Your Life with Croutons

And my life is filled with
frivolous things that are
important to me. If a salad
doesn't have croutons I won't
eat it. I like the crunch of it
the texture of lettuce bark
and brittle brick; these cubist
pieces of burst compliment.
Tender Buttons. Unproven
outlines. My gums rise
a little more, from my teeth
the bite of me is becoming
a frivolous thing. Tender.

Backpacking for Shut-Ins

I pack lightly and carry a big wit

the only option being an introvert

who lacks basic skills of survival

like talking or connecting or finding

bonds through body, kind and spirit

but this imaginary hippopotamus with the violin

is banging out my tune and the only distance

in my voice is what song brings

choir ready to carry a journey

from one side of the room

to another side

of the room

melody

voices

reason

swallow

panic

rebuild

this

pillow

fort

tightly.

6 Ways to Fuck Up Before Breakfast

1. Smoke a joint before you go back to sleep.
   Dream about waking up. Don't.
   When you finally wake up, write.
2. Eat cereal. Vote Fruit Loops. Smoke
   another joint. Vote Cocoa Puffs. Send
   an angry email to your ex. Start
   a list and never finish.
3. Take another shot of whisky. Have a Heineken.
   Send an apologetic email to your ex and let them
   know how you can't live without them. Claim it
   can never get any better than this.
4. Write a poem about how it has
   gotten so much better than this.
5. Make sure to call out of work
   and blame it on your kids
   even if you don't have any.
6. Children are a great excuse.
   Do another line. Blame
   your parents. Watch the sun

                                                go

                              up.

There's Big Money in Staying Put

A point
never
to be
mapped

unravel
my mother
her psychiatrist
said, that I should be

left at home
but my mother
always needed
me

to sleep
on her bedroom
floor every night
until I was 11

I was never the man
of the house nor
did one exist
within

discovery
is for the birds
feeding them song
we are for the pigeons

singing them crackers
not making any
currentcy, pulling
on all these arteries

my mother
helped me
to never leave
her psychiatry.

64 Good Reasons for Giving Up Hope

The only reason to give up hope is to garden.

The only time it is good to garden is
when preparing for the apocalypse.

The only good time for the apocalypse is Jesus.

The only Jesus I know is sold on little wooden
tables in front of dreams on Canal Street.

The only dreams I subscribe to are the ones I am paying for.

The only thing I pay for is this.

The only poetry I write begins with gardens.

The only gardening I do is when I give up.

Controlling Fear Without Getting Frightened

The stuffed elephant
in the room is a way
out sometimes.

When I was lost
amongst the savage
I remember how

a thigh could taste
in someone else's
hands.

The stuffed elephant
in the room
a ceremony of scars

shimmer just enough
that you see them in
everything you hold

or refuse to.

How to Give Yourself A Complete Physical Without Getting Undressed

give yourself a mental pat down

to understand the body's scars physically

play chutes and ladders sliding through

emotions climbing up branched

by past lovers who pass through

every night and hum a sweet silence

but tonight, you are sweet silence through

someone else's past climbing

and whispering through

Famous People Who Were Wiry

The taller they are the harder they are to climb. Branch by branch ladder shaped body descends as I ascend balloon hand ready to receive the sky in all its surround. The thunder clouds become fucked up speakers score the noise my brain trumpets. One of the voices in my head is mute but plays piano constantly with its fists, elbows and feet.

**Peace of Mind by Losing
Complete Control
For 16 Hours a Day**

rose-growled-silver-
streaks-strut-stretched-nylon-
sanity proves the point-
less demeanor is all I've got,
it's all I know, when the kettle
blooms hot, the flame
fuels itself raw, ember'd

some days I can't
remember what I said
or why I said it
or how badly it hurt
someone else
until they forget
what they were feeling
until feeling is liquid
and losing forward

I Suck-You Suck

the poison right

from these teeth

marks, the ghost

from out of

and spirit

upon spindle

dances threaded

light into the room.

We put our best forward.

600 Ways to Give People the Shaft

we wore yellow

to each other's farewell

although the band played

while the dead danced

we morphed

into an unknown

knowing we would

Apartment Hunting for Devil Worshipers

They say to understand the mountain
I must first learn to climb it. Grief
however, is a bottom all to its own
and no matter the climb down
can't help but look up at what
was desired but never gained,
so, I find myself in something else's
worship and share what is often
and fond and new and the embrace
for community is always
piercing, peeling back skin
this neck, this erupture
new, beating and red
it's a mountain, this grief
it's always there.

Only pets allowed.

How to Fillet a Panda

Large black circles
around the eyes gut
through me as I slice
through me this knife
wedges into me like
silk through a needle
sewing open this stab-
ility of consecutive days
without sleep so I lay
on this cutting board
waiting for night to shiv
through me like recipe
I am a delicate feast
for you, your teeth,
in-between them
I rest.

Rid Yourself of Doubt...Or Should You?

I am a tornado.
Within this tornado
I rise. I look up

to myself
when there is nothing
to look up to, lacking

a certain sense
of me like paint-
ings cropped

onto brochures
I don't believe in me
is the only thing

I have been told
to ground myself in, stay present
in the moment but what's a moment

without wings? I am not a plane.
I am more like the runway.
They say balance the negative

with the positive but these critical
gremlins funking inside of me gnaw
on the seesaw, I nurture myself, trying

to forgo myself into harm but I am
the fuel, I don't know how to love
myself yet I know how to

put my needs above everyone else's
I am the fuel, make connections
connect with others, find that spot

on the map that doesn't tell you
where you are yet, when I am
overwhelmed I take a break

punch out my card, bask in
the morning the sun makes.
I am the runway.

**Cooking for The Paralyzed
or
Helping my mother remember her body**

Something
inside you
is trapped.

The pulse
once real
now shaken
everyday
trying to
shake everyday
back into existence.

You haven't lost
your marbles
just the ability
to roll them.

You are an ostrich
with no land
to claim for burial,
you are a funnel
that starts so grand
then becomes so I
am a point on the map
you can no longer find.

I am no longer the map.

You are no longer
the compass.

But you still spin.

I need
that kind
of direction
in my life.

Maybe pasta
with garlic,
red sauce
and a splash
of gin.

A Complete List of All the Things That Are Still Pending

I've often tried to find ways
to end it, to give reason to cause
and reason to claws, this sinister
a rainbow of vein-pump-
muster-spit, this ceremony

for one
to die
as two

finding
emotion
in breath
perceived as
dream and waking
to find it was song

A Treasury of Poorly Understood Ideas

The gold of me is stupid

I can't forget how useless I am

I hold my mediocre

up

to the ground

the latitude

of it all

the distance

it will take me

to understand

the distance

inside of me

full of

Your Shoes Are Worth Money

When someone offers their 2 cents
let them know your time is worth more
than that.

When someone says you haven't walked
a mile in my shoes offer them 2 cents.

Things No One Can Help

The ocean

        is going

        to help

        itself

and that's

        ok.

        Recede.

        Listen.

And that's

        the ocean

        and it should

        be the ocean

but, what

        about me

        is it too

        late, to care

about

        me, the ocean

        is a yawn

        away from

being

        about me.

        I am about

        me. I Recede.

Listen.

How To Turn Unbearable Pain Into Extra Income

Poetry

pulped

from the finest

oranges on mirth

all of them singing in

waves of amber and grainy

light home movies become standard

the real is over the piano boldly pungent

trying to 'toxicate and we go back to my place

but I don't invite you in; I put on my robe then I take it off

I dance around the room alone and then I take out my asthma inhaler;

this unbearable income makes this extra pain more unbearable yet

all

these

oranges.

A Complete List of Everyone's Personal Effects

If at first you don't succeed

Buy a flame thrower

Wave lightening brilliance

In through the outdoor and onto the patio

There was that one time, when, and then, but I just

Breathe deep from pails of sky

Watch the once burned to a crescent tip

Everyone makes a big deal about the moon

I don't know what all the fuss is about

It's just a rock

Orbiting

Trying

To drift

Away

Silent

I Gave Up Hope and Died and It Worked!

You can succeed at dying by giving
what you need most in order to pass
the savings onto someone else
who may need a few more pennies
in the bank when the brick shatters
the body with contrast and ghost
becomes blood, bluer as red
to collage and dye from the inside
looking the same as the person

who gave

up hope

before you

and it worked.

Why Hawaii and Norway Are Not Near Each Other

Shake existence back into these hips,
it starts with distance and ends in dance.

Fill these lungs with tap shoes, one
swollen lymph node, two; shake existence

back into fear and calm are not near
each other but I understand

anxiety, that shitty piece of land
no one wants to build upon except

parking lots and off-track betting.
It starts with dance and ends

in distance, they found something
inside my chest. It's not a heart.

THANK YOU:

M.A. Dennis, thank you for helping me edit this book

Julie, thank you for always providing what my words want to draw

Kristopher, thank you for always making me look pretty

For those not mentioned, you have a place in my heart and in my poems

To George Carlin, thank you for always being a constant muse

To my anxiety, thank you for always being a constant muse

www.ingramcontent.com/pod-product-compliance
Lightning Source LLC
LaVergne TN
LVHW041558070426
835507LV00011B/1158